the
Gin
cookbook

COCKTAILS, CAKES,
DINNERS & DESSERTS

THE PERFECT TONIC
FOR COOKING WITH A

Twist!

 CookNation

the Gin cookbook

COCKTAILS, CAKES, DINNERS & DESSERTS. THE PERFECT TONIC FOR COOKING WITH A TWIST!

ISBN 978-1-912511-69-3

Disclaimer

This book is designed to provide information on cakes & bakes, drinks and meals that can be made using gin as an ingredient.
Some recipes may contain nuts or traces of nuts. Those suffering from any allergies associated with nuts should avoid any recipes containing nuts or nut based oils.
This information is provided and sold with the knowledge that the publisher and author do not offer any legal or other professional advice.
In the case of a need for any such expertise consult with the appropriate professional.
This book does not contain all information available on the subject, and other sources of recipes are available.
Every effort has been made to make this book as accurate as possible. However, there may be typographical and or content errors. Therefore, this book should serve only as a general guide and not as the ultimate source of subject information.
This book contains information that might be dated and is intended only to educate and entertain.
The author and publisher shall have no liability or responsibility to any person or entity regarding any loss or damage incurred, or alleged to have incurred, directly or indirectly, by the information contained in this book.

Contents

Introduction 7

GIN *Savoury Meals, Snacks & Sides* 9

Homemade Gin Burgers 10
Gin Infused Relish 11
Gin & Lemon Chicken 12
Gin Salmon Gravlax 13
Gin & Tonic Pickles 14
Gin, Tomato & Cannellini Bruschetta 15
Gin & Rosemary Marinated Olives 16
Creamy Gin & Tomato Pasta 17
Cucumber Salad with Gin Dressing 18
Rump Steak with Gin Sauce 19
Gin Tomato Soup 20
Gin & Lime Salmon Canapés 21
Gin, Halloumi & Strawberry Skewers 22
Apricot & Gin Gammon 23
Gin Risotto 24
Gin & Lime Prawns 25
Gin & Oregano Lamb 26
Grilled Corn with Gin & Lime Butter 27
Gin & Tonic Battered Cod 28
Gin & Tonic Buns 29
Gin Margarita Pizza 30
Gin Baked Beans 31
Seared Scallops with Gin & Lemon 32

GIN *Desserts & Sweet Treats* 33

Gin & Tonic Cupcakes	34
Gin & Elderflower Cheesecake	35
Gin, Lemon & Lime Marmalade	36
Blueberry Gin Posset	37
Gin & Lime Fudge	38
Gin & Tonic Ice Lollies	39
Gin & Tonic Cake	40
Gin Chocolate Truffles	41
Rhubarb Gin Sorbet	42
Gin & Lemon Meringue Pie	43
Gin Shortbread Biscuits	44
Gin Eton Mess	45
Sloe Gin Cheesecake	46
Gin & Lemon Scones	47
Gin & Tonic Jellies	48
Gin Popcorn	49
Elderflower Gin Sorbet	50
Gin & Lemon Curd	51
Gin & Tonic Ice Cream	52
Gin Poached Pears	53
Gin Gummy Bears	54

GIN *Cocktails* 55

Classic G&T	56
Sloe Gin	57
Gin Mojito	58
Gin Fizz	59
Gin Elderflower Royale	60
Martini	61

Sloe Gin Spritz	62
Strawberry Gin Lemonade	63
Bramble	64
Bee's Knees	65
Rose Gin Fizz	66
Long Island Iced Tea	67
Earl Grey Martini	68
Ruby Sipper	69
Singapore Sling	70
Gimlet	71
Rhubarb Gin Sour	72
Negroni	73
Monkey Gland	74
Gin Buck	75
Gin Corpse Reviver No. 2	76
Tom Collins	77
Aviation	78
Blueberry Gin Sour	79
Vesper Martini	80
Floradora	81
Strawberry Gin Daiquiri	82
Gin-Gin Mule	83
Blue Lady	84
Colour Changing Gin	85
Pomegranate & Rosemary Gin Fizz	86
Peach G&T	87
Mulled Gin	88
Kiwi Gin Fizz	89
Hibiscus Flower Gin Sour	90
Skittles Gin	91

Bonus *Prosecco Recipes*   **92**

Prosecco Chicken   92

Prosecco & Prawn Risotto   93

Prosecco Turkey Meatballs   94

Prosecco Oysters & Turbot   95

You May Also Enjoy...   **96**

— Gin —

The perfect tonic for cooking with a twist!

Simply made by distilling fermented grain with juniper berries; fragrant and herbal, gin has been revered for centuries. Though always esteemed, Gin has made a particularly strong comeback in recent years to become Britain's favourite spirit, with an incredible 47 million bottles being bought last year.

Unsurprisingly, the G&T is the nation's most popular gin tipple, but the days when this was the most exciting thing you could do with gin are long past. Nowadays, the spirit is used in a huge variety of sweet and savoury dishes, as well as complicated cocktails with ingenious flavour combinations.

Gin's unique botanical taste means that there are many flavours which compliment it, from citrus fruits and berries, to vegetables and herbs. Our recipes see gin in combination with everything from the classic lemon and lime, to elderflower, blueberry, rosemary, oregano, and even rhubarb.

Generally speaking, the higher the quality of gin used in the recipes, the better the results will be. However, everyone has different preferences when it comes to gin, so just use your favourite – or even try them with one of the many flavoured gins available today, which span from Turkish delight to frankincense and myrrh!

A brief history of gin

Gin has a long and colourful past. There is evidence of alcohol being infused with juniper berries as far back as 70 A.D, when it was used for medicinal purposes to treat chest ailments.

The name 'gin' comes from an abbreviation of the Danish word for juniper, 'genever', from when the Dutch began producing the spirit in the 16th Century.

It wasn't until the late 17th Century that gin really took hold in Britain. King William III ascended the throne in England, and introduced tax breaks on distilling spirits, leading to the 'Gin Craze' – a time when it was cheaper for the poor to drink a pint of gin than a pint of beer or clean water, and so they did. This was a dark time in gin's history, with many people becoming helplessly addicted, and stories of people being driven mad by the spirit and harming themselves or others. Gin-addicted women neglecting their babies was common, earning gin the nickname 'Mother's Ruin', which survives to this day.

Then came the Gin Act of 1751, the 8th Gin Act intended to reduce the consumption of gin by increasing taxes and duties on retailers. By the early 19th Century, gin was no longer the cheapest alcohol available, and its popularity waned.

In 1830, gin was given a second chance when a man named Aeneas Coffey introduced a new still that allowed for a much purer, safer gin to be made. Twenty-eight years later, in 1858, the first commercial tonic water was released, as a way to disguise the bitter taste of quinine, used by the British Navy to combat malaria in South East Asia at the time. Before long, the two drinks had been combined, and the classic G&T was born. Gin was again held in high esteem – although not in the mania-inducing way it had been, a century before.

Today, it seems gin is once again 'all the rage', particularly in cocktails and as an ingredient in food. These mouth-watering recipes will show you why!

About CookNation

CookNation is the leading publisher of innovative and practical recipe books for the modern, health conscious cook.

CookNation titles bring together delicious, easy and practical recipes with their unique no nonsense approach - making cooking for diets and healthy eating fast, simple and fun. With a range of #1 best-selling titles - from the innovative 'Skinny' calorie-counted series, to the 5:2 Diet Recipes collection - CookNation recipe books prove that 'Diet' can still mean 'Delicious'!

To browse all CookNation's recipe books visit www.bellmackenzie.com

 **CookNation**

— Gin —

Savoury Meals, Snacks & Sides

Homemade Gin Burgers

Ingredients

- ½ tbsp olive oil
- 1 small onion, finely chopped
- 500g/1lb 2oz beef mince
- ¼ cup breadcrumbs
- ½ tsp dried herbs
- 1 egg

- 2 tbsp gin
- 1 tsp sesame oil
- Salt & black pepper
- 4 white rolls
- Handful lettuce leaves
- Tomato ketchup, to serve

Method

1 Heat the olive oil in a pan over a medium heat. Add the onions and fry until soft.

2 In a large bowl, combine the mince, breadcrumbs and dried herbs.

3 In another bowl, whisk the egg, then add the gin and sesame oil, and season with salt and pepper.

4 Carefully fold the gin mixture into the mince, and add the cooked onion.

5 Shape the mix into 4 burger patties.

6 Heat a griddle pan to a medium-high heat, and cook the burgers for approximately 6 minutes on each side, or until the juices run clear.

7 Remove the burger patties, and lightly toast the inside of the buns on the hot griddle.

8 Serve the burgers in the open buns, with lettuce and ketchup to taste.

These zingy gin burgers can be served with any of your favourite toppings, from mustard to mayonnaise.

Gin Infused Relish

Ingredients

- 1 tsp olive oil
- 1 clove garlic, finely chopped
- ¼ onion, chopped
- ¼ tsp paprika
- ¼ tsp ginger powder
- ¼ tsp mustard seeds

- 100g/3½ oz passata
- 60ml/2floz white vinegar
- 60g/2½ oz sugar
- 1 tsp Worcestershire sauce
- 2 tsp gin

Method

1 Heat the olive oil in a pan over a medium heat. Add the onions and garlic and fry for 5 minutes, until soft.

2 Add the paprika, ginger powder and mustard seeds to the pan, and toast for 2 minutes.

3 Turn the heat down to low, add the passata, vinegar, sugar & Worcestershire sauce and simmer for 15 minutes.

4 Add the gin, cook for 2 more minutes, then remove from heat.

5 Pour the mixture into a food processor and blend until smooth.

6 Allow to cool before serving.

This tangy relish is 'gincredible' served on burgers, with chips, or slathered on crusty bread – an essential addition to your summer BBQ!

Gin & Lemon Chicken

Ingredients

- **60ml/2 floz gin**
- **60ml/2 floz lemon juice**
- **1 tsp salt**
- **1 tsp sugar**
- **½ tsp dried oregano**

- **100ml/3½ floz vegetable oil**
- **4 x large skinless, boneless chicken breasts**
- **4 lemon wedges, to serve**

Method

1 In a dish, mix together the gin, lemon juice, salt, sugar and oregano.

2 Gradually add the vegetable oil, whisking constantly until the mixture is combined.

3 Add the chicken breasts, ensuring they are coated thoroughly, and leave in the fridge to marinate for 30 minutes.

4 Heat a large frying pan or griddle pan over a medium-high heat.

5 Remove the chicken breasts from the marinade and cook in the pan for 15 minutes, turning halfway through, until the juices run clear.

6 Remove the cooked chicken and serve hot with a wedge of lemon on the side.

Serve this tangy chicken with new potatoes and a green side salad for a fresh summertime meal.

Gin Salmon Gravlax

Ingredients

- 2 x 1kg/2¼ lb fresh salmon fillets, bones removed
- 60ml/2 floz gin
- 10 juniper berries
- 225g/8oz salt

- 150g/5oz sugar
- 1 tbsp black pepper
- 1 tbsp dill seeds
- 1 tbsp coriander seeds
- 150g/5oz fresh dill, chopped

Method

1 Line a large baking tray with tin foil and lay the salmon fillets in it, skin-side down.

2 Pour the gin evenly over the salmon.

3 In a small bowl, lightly crush the juniper berries and poon onto the salmon fillets. Press to ensure they stay in place.

4 In another bowl, mix the salt, sugar and black pepper until combined.

5 Grind the dill and coriander seeds with a pestle and mortar, add to the salt mixture, and combine. Sprinkle this mixture over the salmon fillets.

6 Cover the salmon fillets with aluminium foil. Place another baking tray on top and weigh down to compress the fish.

7 Chill in the fridge for 3 days.

8 To serve, unwrap the salmon and wipe off the seasoning and juniper berries. Slice the fillets diagonally into 80+ fine slices, sprinkle with dill, and serve.

Serve this mouth-watering dish with rye bread and homemade cucumber relish!

Gin & Tonic Pickles

Serves 4

Ingredients

- **6 small cucumbers**
- **175ml/6 floz gin**
- **60ml/2 floz lime juice**
- **1 lime, sliced**
- **175ml/6 floz tonic water**

Method

1 Remove the ends of the cucumbers, and slice them into quarters, lengthways.

2 Place the cucumbers into a jar. Add the gin, lime juice and lime slices, screw on the lid of the jar, and shake.

3 Remove the lid and top up the jar with tonic water, so that the cucumbers are completely submerged.

4 Place the sealed jar in the fridge and leave for 2 days.

5 After 2 days the pickles are ready to eat, and will keep for a month in the fridge.

These boozy pickles are the perfect way to use up the old gin that's been sitting at the back of the cupboard for years. They're perfect in burgers or salads – or enjoyed just on their own!

Gin, Tomato & Cannellini Bruschetta

Ingredients

- 650g/1lb 7oz cherry tomatoes
- 1 tbsp dried basil
- 1 tsp sugar
- 1 tsp salt
- 12 slices ciabatta bread

- 3 tbsp olive oil
- 1 red onion, thinly sliced
- 60ml/2 floz gin
- 400g/14oz cannellini beans, drained

Method

1 Preheat the oven to 200°C/400°F/Gas Mark 6.

2 Grease a large baking tray and lay out the cherry tomatoes.

3 Sprinkle the basil, salt and sugar over the tomatoes. Place them in the oven and roast for 30 minutes, turning half way through.

4 Meanwhile, lightly toast the ciabatta slices and spoon 2 tbsp of the olive oil over them.

5 Heat the remaining 1 tbsp of olive oil in a pan over a medium heat, add the onion, and fry for 3 minutes.

6 Add the roasted tomatoes and gin. Stir in the cannellini beans and cook until warmed through before removing from heat.

7 Spoon the tomato and bean mixture over the ciabatta slices, sprinkle with a pinch more salt, and serve.

Great as a dinner party starter or snack for your cocktail evening – why not ask your guests to guess the secret ingredient?

Gin & Rosemary Marinated Olives

Ingredients

- **120ml/4 floz olive oil**
- **120ml/4 floz gin**
- **2 cloves garlic, finely chopped**
- **Small handful fresh rosemary**
- **275g/10oz mixed olives**

Method

1 Preheat the oven to 180°C/350°F/Gas Mark 4.

2 In a bowl, combine the olive oil, gin, garlic and rosemary.

3 Add the olives, and stir to coat.

4 Place the marinated olives in an oven proof dish, and roast for 25 minutes. Allow to cool before serving.

We think you'll agree these tasty olives are a bit 'moreish'. If you're not a fan of rosemary, replace it with another herb, such as oregano or basil.

Creamy Gin & Tomato Pasta

Ingredients

- 350g/12oz dried pasta
- 60ml/2 floz olive oil
- 1 small onion, finely chopped
- 1 clove garlic, finely chopped
- 120ml/4 floz gin
- 250g/9oz chopped tomatoes
- 250ml/8½ floz double cream
- 1 tsp chopped fresh rosemary
- 1 tsp chilli pepper flakes
- 1 tbsp grated Parmesan

Method

1 Cook the pasta in a large pan of boiling water until al dente.

2 Meanwhile, heat the olive oil in a large pan on a medium heat, and fry the onion and garlic until they start to soften.

3 Pour in the gin, bring to the boil, then simmer for 2 minutes.

4 Reduced the heat. Add the chopped tomatoes, double cream, rosemary and chilli pepper flakes, and very gently simmer for 15 minutes, stirring regularly.

5 Add the cooked, drained pasta to the pan with the sauce, and toss to coat.

6 Stir in the Parmesan cheese, and serve immediately.

This creamy, gin-based sauce is a great alternative to the classic vodka and tomato pasta sauce, and has a more herbal flavour.

Cucumber Salad with Gin Dressing

Ingredients

- **2 cucumbers**
- **4 cherry tomatoes**
- **60ml/2 floz gin**
- **60ml/2floz fresh lemon juice**

- **120ml/4 floz olive oil**
- **Salt & pepper**
- **Handful fresh flat leaf parsley**

Method

1 Cut the cucumber into long, thin slices, and arrange on a serving plate.

2 Slice the tomatoes into wedges, and scatter them over the cucumber slices.

3 Finely chop the parsley.

4 In a separate bowl, whisk together the gin, lemon juice, olive oil and a pinch of salt and pepper.

5 Pour the dressing over the cucumber and tomato salad, garnish with the chopped parsley, and serve over crispy green salad leaves.

Was there ever a more perfect pairing than gin and cucumber? Give this simple salad a go, and find out!

Rump Steak with Gin Sauce

Ingredients

- 4 tsp juniper berries, lightly crushed
- 1 tsp peppercorns
- ½ tsp salt
- ½ tsp coriander seeds
- 2 tbsp olive oil

- 1kg/2¼ lb rump steak, approx. 5cm thick
- 250ml/8½ floz beef stock
- 2 sprigs rosemary
- 100ml/3½ floz double cream
- 60ml/2 floz gin

Method

1 Using a pestle and mortar, grind together 2 tsp of juniper berries, the peppercorns, salt and coriander seeds to form a powder.

2 Coat the steak with the olive oil, then rub with the powder. Leave to marinate for 30 minutes.

3 Meanwhile, make the sauce by adding the beef stock, rosemary and remaining 2 tsp of juniper berries to a saucepan and bringing to the boil. Simmer until the stock has reduced by half.

4 Sieve the mixture into a clean pan. Add the double cream & gin and warm through.

5 Heat another pan on a high heat, then add the marinated steak and cook for 4-6 minutes on each side, according to your preferences.

6 Remove from the heat and allow to rest for 5 minutes, before serving with the warm gin sauce.

For a light summer meal enjoy with a rocket salad. In winter, it goes well with potatoes, vegetables and all the trimmings.

Serves 4

Gin Tomato Soup

Ingredients

- 25ml/1 floz olive oil
- 1 clove garlic, finely chopped
- 2 leeks, chopped
- 1 carrot, sliced
- 1 tsp dried basil
- 1 tsp dried oregano
- 1 tsp salt

- 1 bay leaf
- 15g/½ oz flour
- 750ml/1¼ pints vegetable stock
- 1 litre/1½ pints gin
- 6 tomatoes, chopped
- Crème fraiche, to serve

Method

1 Heat the oil in a large pan over a medium heat, add the garlic and leeks, and cook until they begin to soften.

2 Add the carrot, basil, oregano, salt, bay leaf and flour. Stir and simmer for 10 minutes.

3 Pour in the vegetable stock, gin and chopped tomatoes. Bring to the boil and simmer for a further 30 minutes.

4 Sieve the soup, then ladle into bowls and serve garnished with crème fraiche.

A modern take on a classic dish, enjoy this delicious soup with crusty bread for the ultimate comfort food.

Gin & Lime Salmon Canapés

Serves 9

Ingredients

- **45ml/1½ floz gin**
- **1 lime, grated for the rind**
- **1 tbsp salt**
- **1 tbsp peppercorns**
- **175g/6oz fresh salmon fillets, bones and skin removed**

- **175g/6oz sushi rice**
- **15g/½oz sugar**
- **2 tbsp rice vinegar**
- **18 slices pickled ginger**
- **1 tbsp wasabi paste**

Method

1 In a bowl, mix together the gin, lime rind, salt and peppercorns to make a marinade.

2 Lay the salmon fillets in the marinade and chill in the fridge overnight.

3 Add the sushi rice to a pan with 420ml/14½ floz of water, bring to the boil, then simmer and cook for 10 minutes or until the liquid has all evaporated.

4 Stir the sugar and rice vinegar into the cooked rice. Remove from heat and allow to cool.

5 Cut the salmon into 36 thin slices.

6 Assemble the canapés by moulding the sushi rice into 18 evenly sized balls, adding 2 slices of salmon, a slice of pickled ginger and a dash of wasabi paste on top.

These spicy canapés are the perfect start to a dinner party, wedding buffet or other special occasion.

Gin, Halloumi & Strawberry Skewers

Ingredients

- **25ml/1 floz gin**
- **60ml/2 floz olive oil**
- **Handful fresh mint leaves, chopped**

- **250g/9oz halloumi, cubed**
- **2 courgettes, trimmed and thickly sliced**
- **400g/14oz strawberries**

Method

1 In a bowl, mix the gin, 45ml of the olive oil and the mint leaves to form the dressing.

2 Assemble the skewers by threading alternating slices of halloumi, courgette and strawberries onto 12 skewers.

3 Heat a large griddle pan, place the skewers in and drizzle over the remaining olive oil. Sear each skewer for 2 minutes, turning halfway through, until the halloumi starts to turn golden.

4 Serve the skewers drizzled with the gin and mint dressing.

5 Tip: Precook the courgettes for a little while before assembling the skewers if you prefer them tender.

Serve these summery skewers with rosé wine or Pimm's and lemonade - they make a fabulous vegetarian option at a BBQ.

Apricot & Gin Gammon

Ingredients

- 25ml/1 floz gin
- 1 tbsp apricot jam
- 2 x 225g/8oz gammon steaks
- 40g/1½ oz butter, softened
- 1 tbsp chopped parsley
- 25g/1oz dried apricots, finely chopped
- Juice of ½ a lemon

Method

1 In a small bowl, mix together the gin and apricot jam. Use to glaze the gammon steaks, and set aside.

2 In another bowl combine together the butter, parsley, dried apricots and lemon juice.

3 Grill the gammon steaks over a high heat for 3 minutes on each side, then serve with the apricot butter.

These sticky gin gammon steaks are a sophisticated treat, and the fruity apricot adds an interesting twist.

Gin Risotto

Ingredients

- 15ml/½ floz olive oil
- 1 onion, chopped
- 1 clove garlic, finely chopped
- 2 carrots, chopped
- 1 leek, chopped
- 1 red pepper, chopped

- 300g/11oz risotto rice
- 75ml/2½ fl oz gin
- 1 litre/1½ pints vegetable stock
- 1 tbsp butter
- 1 tbsp Parmesan cheese
- Salt & black pepper

Method

1 Heat the oil in a large pan over a medium heat. Add the onion, garlic, carrot, leek and red pepper, and fry until the onion is soft.

2 Add the risotto rice, and mix thoroughly.

3 Pour in the gin, stirring continuously, until it is all absorbed.

4 Gradually add the vegetable stock, a little at a time, stirring continuously while the rice simmers for approximately 15 minutes.

5 Once all the stock is gone and the rice is cooked, stir in the butter and Parmesan cheese, season with salt and pepper, and serve.

A gin with strong herbal notes works well in this dish, but you can experiment with different brands and flavours to find your perfect recipe.

Gin & Lime Prawns

Ingredients

- **4 limes**
- **60ml/2floz gin**
- **15ml/½ floz olive oil**
- **½ tsp chilli flakes**

- **1 clove garlic, finely chopped**
- **Handful coriander**
- **40 large king prawns**

Method

1 Grate and juice 2 of the limes.

2 Add the zest and juice to a bowl along with the gin, olive oil, chilli flakes, garlic and coriander. Mix well to create a marinade.

3 Lay the prawns in the marinade, then leave in the fridge to infuse overnight.

4 Heat a frying pan over a medium high heat. Cook the prawns for 3 minutes, until pink and cooked through.

5 Slice the remaining 2 limes into wedges, and serve with the cooked prawns.

Great as a sharing platter, serve these tangy prawns with bread and salad for a true seafood feast!

Gin & Oregano Lamb

Ingredients

- **60ml/2floz gin**
- **60ml/2floz olive oil**
- **1 onion, peeled**
- **1 apple, de-cored**
- **Juice of 1 lemon**

- **1 tsp salt**
- **1 tsp peppercorns**
- **Handful fresh oregano, chopped**
- **1.5kg/3lb 6oz lamb leg or shoulder**

Method

1 Add the gin, olive oil, onion, apple, lemon, salt and pepper to a food processor and blend until smooth to make a paste/sauce.

2 Stir in the chopped oregano. Apply the marinade paste to the lamb and leave in a large, sealed food bag or wrapped in tin foil to chill in the fridge overnight.

3 Preheat the oven to 200°C/400°F/Gas Mark 6.

4 Remove the lamb from the fridge and place in a roasting dish. Pour any remaining marinade over the lamb.

5 Roast in the oven for approximately 90 minutes (less if you like it medium-rare or rare).

6 Once cooked, remove from the oven and allow to rest for 10 minutes, before serving.

Serve this fragrant lamb as part of your Sunday roast, or carve it into slices and make sandwiches – they are delicious with a blackberry sauce.

Grilled Corn with Gin & Lime Butter

Ingredients

- **8 whole ears of corn (large corn on the cob)**
- **125g/4oz butter**
- **1 tsp gin**
- **1 tsp lime juice**
- **2 cloves garlic, finely chopped**
- **Pinch salt**

Method

1 Preheat the oven to 200°C/400°F/Gas Mark 6.

2 In a bowl, mix together the butter, gin, lime juice and garlic.

3 Massage each ear of corn with the gin butter mix, then wrap each one in a piece of tin foil.

4 Bake in the oven for 30 minutes, or until tender.

5 Serve whilst hot and buttery.

You can also cook these delicious gin grilled corns on the barbecue. They are the perfect accompaniment to lemon chicken.

Gin & Tonic Battered Cod

Ingredients

- 7g/¼ oz fresh yeast
- Pinch salt
- Pinch sugar
- 100ml/3½ floz tonic water
- 15ml/½ floz gin
- 100g/3½ oz plain flour
- ½ tsp cider vinegar
- Vegetable oil, for frying
- 2 x 175/6oz skinless, boneless cod fillets
- Salt and pepper
- Lemon wedges, to serve

Method

1 In a bowl, combine the yeast with a pinch of salt and sugar.

2 Add the tonic water, then whisk in the gin, flour and cider vinegar. Leave until the mixture starts to bubble.

3 Heat the oil in a pan over a medium-high heat.

4 Coat the cod fillets in the bubbling batter, then fry in the pan for 4 minutes, turning halfway through.

5 Remove the battered cod and allow to drain on kitchen paper.

6 Season with salt and pepper, then serve the crispy fish hot, with lemon wedges on the side.

Here, gin makes an interesting alternative to the traditional beer-battered cod. Delicious with homemade chips and tartar sauce!

Gin & Tonic Buns

Ingredients

- 50ml/2floz tonic
- 75g/3oz sultanas
- 75ml/3floz gin
- 100ml/3 ½ floz milk
- 30g/1oz butter
- 75ml/3 floz cold water

- 350g/12oz strong white bread flour
- Large punch salt
- 7g sachet fast action dried yeast
- 2 tbsp sugar
- ½ tsp mixed spice

Method

1 Place the sultanas in the gin & tonic and leave to soak overnight. In the morning place on kitchen towels to dry off a little.

2 Sift the flour, yeast, sugar, spice & salt into a large bowl.

3 Gently melt the butter in a pan with the milk. Remove from the heat and stir in the cool water. When cooled to room temperature gently combine the butter into the sifted flour and mix together to form a dough. Flour a flat surface and knead for a few minutes.

4 Place in a bowl, cover and allow to proof at room temperature for an hour (or until it doubles in size).

5 Pre-heat the oven to 200C/180C fan/ gas mark 6.

6 Remove dough from the bowl and gently kneed in the gin soaked sultanas.

7 Divide the dough into 6 even-sized pieces and roll into balls. Place on a non stick baking tray and gently flatten with your palm to make teacake shaped buns.

8 Place in the oven and bake for 20-25 mins or until the buns are golden and risen.

9 Allow to cool on a wire rack and serve.

Gin Margarita Pizza

Ingredients

- **75ml/2½ fl oz olive oil**
- **250ml/8½ fl oz water**
- **2 tsp salt**
- **1 tbsp dry yeast**
- **425g/15oz high gluten flour**
- **1 onion, finely diced**
- **2 cloves garlic, finely diced**

- **1 tsp dried oregano**
- **½ tsp dried chilli flakes**
- **250g/9oz tinned peeled tomatoes**
- **250ml/8½ fl oz double cream**
- **100ml/3½ fl oz gin**
- **150g/5oz fresh mozzarella, torn**
- **6 fresh basil leaves**

Method

1 Preheat the oven to 225°C/450°F/Gas 8, or as high as your oven with allow.

2 In a large bowl, combine 60ml/2 fl oz of the olive oil with the water, salt and dry yeast. Gradually mix in the flour to form a dough.

3 Shape the dough into a ball, cover the bowl with a tea towel, and set aside to proof for 1 hour.

4 Meanwhile, heat the remaining tbsp of olive oil in a large pan. Add the onion, and cook for 5 mins. Add the garlic, oregano, chilli flakes & tomatoes. Bring to the boil, simmer and stir on a medium heat for 15 mins.

5 Add the cream and simmer for another 15 minutes. Stir in the gin, and cook for a further 5 minutes. Remove sauce from heat and blend in a food processor until smooth.

6 Make the pizza by stretching the proofed dough into a large disc 30cm in diameter. Cover with a thick layer of the sauce and scatter with the mozzarella.

7 Cook in the pre-heated oven for 8-10 mins or until the cheese has melted and the base is cooked through. Remove from the oven, top with the fresh basil leaves and a drizzle of olive oil to serve.

Gin Baked Beans

Ingredients

- **2 x 400g/14oz tins baked beans**
- **15ml/½ floz olive oil**
- **1 onion, finely diced**
- **2 cloves garlic, finely diced**
- **300ml/10½ floz tomato ketchup**
- **60g/2½ oz brown sugar**
- **125g/4oz molasses**
- **1 tbsp chilli powder**
- **1 tsp mustard powder**
- **1 tsp Liquid Smoke**
- **120ml/4 floz gin**

Method

1 Preheat the oven to 170°C/325°F/Gas Mark 3.

2 Place the baked beans into a large casserole dish.

3 Heat the olive oil in a pan over a medium heat and fry the onion and garlic until softened. Then, add to the casserole dish.

4 Add all the remaining ingredients (except the gin) to the casserole dish and stir well.

5 Bake in the oven for 30 minutes, until a crust begins to form. Stir the beans well, then bake for a further 30 mins, stirring regularly.

6 Pour in the gin, stir to combine and bake for a final 30 minutes.

7 Remove from the oven and leave to stand for 10 minutes before serving.

There are a couple of ingredients here that you are unlikely to have already, but are worth tracking down. Liquid Smoke adds a delicious (and vegan!) BBQ flavour to any meal.

Seared Scallops with Gin & Lemon

Ingredients

- **12 large sea scallops**
- **Salt & black pepper**
- **25ml/1 floz olive oil**
- **60ml/2fl oz gin**

- **60ml/2 fl oz lemon juice**
- **15ml/½ fl oz orange juice**
- **75g/3oz unsalted butter, cubed**

Method

1 Heat the olive oil in a large pan over a medium-high heat.

2 Add the scallops, season with salt and pepper, and quickly sear on each side for 2 minutes, until the surface of each starts to brown.

3 Remove the scallops to a plate to cool.

4 Add the gin, lemon and orange juice to the pan. Bring to the boil, then simmer on a low heat.

5 Gradually add the cubes of butter, whisking continuously as you do, to form a thick, creamy sauce.

6 Add the scallops and their juices back into the pan and stir to coat with the sauce. Serve immediately.

More commonly cooked in white wine, using gin in this recipe instead really highlights the citrusy notes. Serve with tarragon or samphire as a starter, or with linguine as a main course.

— Gin —
Desserts & Sweet Treats

Gin & Tonic Cupcakes

Ingredients

- **400g/14oz unsalted butter**
- **250g/9oz caster sugar**
- **200g/7oz self-raising flour**
- **4 eggs, beaten**
- **150ml/5 floz gin**

- **60ml/2 fl oz tonic water**
- **2 limes, 1 finely grated for zest, 1 cut into tiny wedges for decoration**

Method

1 Preheat the oven to 180°C/350°F/ Gas Mark 4. Prepare a cake tray with 12 cupcake cases.

2 In a large bowl, beat 200g butter with 200g sugar. Add the self-raising flour and eggs, and mix until combined. Fold in 75ml of gin.

3 Divide the cake batter between the 12 cupcake cases and bake in the oven for 20-25 mins or until risen & golden.

4 Meanwhile, make a gin and tonic syrup by bringing to the boil the remaining 50g of sugar and 50ml of tonic water until the sugar dissolves. Then, stir in 30ml gin.

5 Brush the gin syrup over the cupcakes as soon as they come out of the oven. Leave to stand for 10 minutes, transfer to a wire rack and allow to cool completely.

6 Make the buttercream by whisking the remaining 200g of butter until soft, and then slowly beat in the icing sugar until thick and creamy. Add the last 45ml of gin gradually, beating continuously.

7 Decorate the cooled cupcakes by adding a spoonful of buttercream to the top of each, followed by a lime wedge and a sprinkling of lime zest.

Gin & Elderflower Cheesecake

Ingredients

- 275g/10oz digestive biscuits
- 100g/3½ oz butter, melted
- 600g/1lb 5oz cream cheese
- 100g/3½ oz icing sugar
- 275ml/9½ floz double cream
- 60ml/2fl oz gin
- 250ml/8½ floz pre-mixed gin and elderflower tonic
- 2tbsp caster sugar
- 1 lemon, ½ juiced, ½ sliced
- 3 tbsp elderflower cordial

Method

1 Blitz the biscuits in a food processor to make crumbs. Place the crumbed biscuits into a bowl, add the melted butter and mix.

2 Grease a round baking tin (with a removable base) and line with parchment paper. Tip the biscuit crumbs in and press down firmly to form a cheesecake base. Refrigerate for 1 hour, or until set.

3 Combine the cream cheese and icing sugar into a bowl. Whisk until smooth. Add the gin and cream, and continue whisking until thick and smooth.

4 Spoon the mixture over the cheesecake base. Use a spatula to spread evenly. Refrigerate overnight.

5 Pour the pre-mixed gin and elderflower tonic into a pan and add the caster sugar & lemon juice. Bring to the boil and reduce over a high heat for 4 minutes, until a syrup forms.

6 Remove from the heat. Stir in the elderflower cordial and allow the mixture to cool completely.

7 Carefully remove the cheesecake from the baking tin, pour over the elderflower syrup, decorate with the lemon slices, and serve.

Gin, Lemon & Lime Marmalade

Ingredients

- **7 limes**
- **60ml/2 floz lemon juice**
- **500ml/17 floz water**

- **800g/1¾ lb sugar**
- **60ml/2 floz gin**

Method

1 Cut all the limes in half and juice them into a bowl. Scrape the remaining lime membranes and pips into a separate bowl. Chop finely, then place on top of a muslin square. Gather and tie the corners with string to make a membrane-filled parcel. Place this in a large pan.

2 Finely slice the lime peels, then add these to the pan, along with the lemon juice and water. Leave the mixture to soak overnight.

3 In the morning, bring the pan to the boil over a medium-high heat, and then leave to simmer for 2 hours.

4 Remove the muslin parcel, squeeze out any excess lime juice and discard.

5 Add the sugar and stir until fully dissolved. Bring the mixture back to the boil, and cook until it reaches setting point. After 20 minutes, test it by inserting a wooden spoon. If some of the mixture sticks to the spoon when it is removed, the jam is ready.

6 Gently stir in the gin, then ladle the jam into 4 sterilised glass mason jars, seal and allow to cool completely before labelling or serving.

Blueberry Gin Posset

Ingredients

- **275g/10oz frozen blueberries**
- **60ml/2 floz gin**
- **400ml/14 floz double cream**

- **100g/3½ oz caster sugar**
- **12 fresh blueberries**

Method

1 Place the frozen blueberries and gin in food processor, and blend.

2 Sieve the mixture to ensure it is perfectly smooth.

3 Place the double cream and sugar in a pan over a low heat, and warm until the sugar dissolves.

4 Gradually increase the heat, then boil for 2 minutes, stirring continuously.

5 Remove from the heat and fold in the blueberry gin.

6 Allow to cool for 10 minutes, then spoon the mixture into 4 small glasses.

7 Chill in the fridge for at least 2 hours, until set.

8 Sprinkle each posset with 3 blueberries, and serve.

Blueberry pairs well with gin, but you could also try this delicious posset with raspberries, blackberries or strawberries (or a mix of all 3!)

Gin & Lime Fudge

Ingredients

- **400g/14oz condensed milk**
- **800g/1¾ lb white chocolate, chopped**
- **Pinch salt**

- **75ml/2½ floz gin**
- **25ml/1 floz fresh lime juice**
- **Zest of 2 limes**

Method

1 Line a brownie tin with parchment paper.

2 Heat the condensed milk, white chocolate and a pinch of salt gently in a saucepan, stirring continuously until the chocolate has fully melted.

3 Add the gin, lime juice and lime zest, and stir to combine.

4 Pour the mixture into the pre-lined tin, smooth out evenly and top with another sprinkling of lime zest.

5 Leave to chill in the fridge overnight. Once set, cut the fudge into (approximately 40) cubes, and enjoy!

The combination of botanical gin, zesty lime and sweet white chocolate makes this a decadent treat you won't want to share!

Gin & Tonic Ice Lollies

Ingredients

(Based on 10 x 100ml ice lolly moulds)
- **200ml/7 floz gin**
- **Juice of 2 lemons**
- **750ml/1¼ pint tonic, flat**

- **60ml/2 fl oz sugar syrup (equal parts sugar and water)**
- **1 lemon, thinly sliced**

Method

1 In a bowl, mix the gin, tonic, sugar syrup and lemon juice together.

2 Divide the mixture evenly between your ice lolly moulds.

3 Add a thin slice of lemon and a lolly stick to each mould.

4 Leave in the freezer overnight, then serve.

These lollies are best enjoyed on hot summer nights (or when you've had a rough day!) Adjust the amount of gin and tonic depending on the size of your moulds, or how strong you like your G&Ts.

Gin & Tonic Cake

Ingredients

- **450g/1lb unsalted butter**
- **375g/13oz caster sugar**
- **250g/9oz self raising flour**
- **5 eggs**
- **3 limes, zested and cut into wedges**

- **Juice of 1 lime**
- **150ml tonic water**
- **1 tsp juniper berries, crushed**
- **60ml/2 floz gin**
- **400g icing sugar**

Method

1 Grease a 2lb cake tin and preheat the oven to 180°C/350°F/Gas Mark 4.

2 In a bowl, beat together 250g of the butter with 250g of sugar, until creamed. Add the flour, eggs and zest of 1 lime, and mix well.

3 Pour the mix into the cake tin, and bake for 35-40 minutes, or until a skewer poked in the centre emerges clean.

4 Meanwhile make the syrup by heating the remaining sugar, lime juice, tonic & berries on a medium heat, stirring continuously. Once the sugar dissolves boil for 5 mins until a syrup forms. Sieve the syrup then mix in 30ml of the gin.

5 Remove the cake from the oven. Allow to cool for 5 mins, poke holes in it with a skewer and drizzle the syrup over.

6 Make the buttercream icing by gradually beating the icing sugar into the remaining 200g of butter. Once creamed, fold in the last 30ml of gin, and zest of the 2nd lime.

7 Allow the cake to fully cool then spread the butter icing evenly over the top and sides using a flat knife.

8 Decorate with the remaining lime zest, and lime wedges, and serve.

Gin Chocolate Truffles

Ingredients

- 200g/7oz dark chocolate
- 60ml/2 floz double cream
- 100g/3½ oz butter, cubed
- 60ml/2 floz gin
- Juice of 1 lime
- Cocoa powder, to serve

Method

1 Break the chocolate into small pieces, then place it in a heatproof bowl with the double cream, and mix.

2 Place the bowl on top of a saucepan of simmering water, and heat gently until the chocolate melts.

3 Fold in the butter, gin and lime juice and whisk until smooth.

4 Place in a sealed container and leave to cool in the fridge overnight.

5 Take teaspoons of the mixture and carefully roll into truffle-sized balls (approx. 40).

6 Dust with the cocoa powder, and serve.

These alcoholic truffles are great as a Christmas treat, wedding favours, or as a homemade gift for family and friends.

Rhubarb Gin Sorbet

Ingredients

- 275g/10oz caster sugar
- 100ml/3½ floz water
- Juice of 1 lemon

- 600g/1lb 5oz rhubarb, trimmed and finely chopped
- 100ml/3½ fl oz gin

Method

1 In a large pan heat the sugar and water over a medium heat until the sugar dissolves.

2 Add the rhubarb and lemon juice, increase the heat and simmer until the rhubarb is tender and falling apart.

3 Blend in a food processor until the mixture is completely smooth. Transfer to a shallow, wide container and refrigerate for 1 hour.

4 Stir in the gin. Place the container in the freezer and freeze for 1 hour.

5 Remove from the freezer. Whisk the sorbet, then place back in the freezer for 30 minutes. Repeat this process 5-6 times, until the mixture is too thick to whisk.

6 Cover and freeze overnight – your sorbet is then ready to enjoy.

The gin in this tangy sorbet accentuates the floral, tart flavour of the rhubarb

Gin & Lemon Meringue Pie

Ingredients

- **200g/7oz caster sugar**
- **1 tbsp plain flour**
- **25g/1oz cornflour**
- **Pinch salt**
- **300ml/10½ floz water**
- **Juice and zest of 2 lemons**
- **25g/1oz butter, cubed**
- **4 egg yolks, beaten**
- **60ml/2 floz gin**
- **1 shortcrust pastry case, pre-baked**
- **4 egg whites**

Method

1 Preheat the oven to 180°C/350°F/Gas Mark 4.

2 In a pan, mix together 200g of sugar, the flour, cornflour and a pinch of salt.

3 Add the water, lemon and lemon zest.

4 Bring the mixture to the boil, then stir in the butter.

5 Beat in the egg yolks and gin. Simmer for 5 minutes, until the mixture turns thick.

6 Pour the lemon mixture into the pre-baked pastry case.

7 In a separate bowl whisk together the egg whites and remaining 75g of sugar until stick peaks form. Spread the meringue on top of the lemon mixture.

8 Bake in the oven for 15 minutes, then remove and allow to cool fully before serving.

This classic dish is given an adults only twist with a dash of gin, which perfectly compliments the tangy lemon and sweet meringue.

Gin Shortbread Biscuits

Ingredients

- **250g/9oz butter, softened**
- **100g/3½ oz icing sugar**
- **60g/2½ oz flour**

- **125g/4oz cornflour**
- **45ml/1½ floz gin**
- **Juice and zest of 1 lemon**

Method

1 Preheat the oven to 170°C/325°F/Gas Mark 3.

2 In a bowl, mix together the butter and icing sugar. Add the flour and cornflour, and combine. Mix in the gin and lemon juice and form a dough.

3 Roll the dough out using a rolling pin, to an even thickness of approx. 1cm/½".

4 Cut into 10 evenly sized squares. Place squares on a baking tray in the pre-heated oven, and bake for 20 minutes, until golden.

5 Remove from the oven and transfer to a wire rack to cool.

6 Sprinkle with the lemon zest, and serve.

Enjoy these delicious, buttery biscuits with a nice cup of Earl Grey tea – the floral notes compliment the juniper of the gin perfectly.

Gin Eton Mess

Ingredients

- **400g/14oz strawberries**
- **60ml/2 fl oz gin**
- **400ml/14fl oz double cream**
- **1 tbsp caster sugar**
- **4 meringue nests**

Method

1 Take 200g of the strawberries and slice into quarters. Place them in a bowl, pour over the gin, then leave in the fridge to soak overnight.

2 Drain, then blitz the strawberries in food processer, to make a sauce.

3 Whisk the cream and sugar together in a large bowl until it forms soft peaks.

4 Crumble the meringue nests, and fold into the whipped cream.

5 Slice the remaining strawberries, and fold these into the cream/meringue mixture.

6 Divide between 4 glasses, drizzle over the gin and strawberry sauce, and serve immediately.

Could there be anything better than watching Wimbledon with a glass of Prosecco and this gin soaked strawberry Eton Mess? We think not.

Sloe Gin Cheesecake

Ingredients

- 250g/9oz digestive biscuits
- 125g/4oz unsalted butter, melted
- 300ml/10½ floz double cream
- 250g/9oz mascarpone
- 275g/10oz cream cheese
- 60g/2½ oz icing sugar
- 1 tsp vanilla extract
- Zest of 1 lemon
- 100ml/3½ floz sloe gin
- 140g/4½ oz blackcurrant jam
- 15ml/½ floz gin

Method

1 Lightly grease an 8" round baking tin with removable base in preparation.

2 Blitz the digestive biscuits in a food processor.

3 Place the crumbed biscuits in a bowl, add the melted butter and mix.

4 Tip into the tin and press down firmly to form the cheesecake base.

5 Refrigerate for 1 hour, or until set.

6 Add the double cream, mascarpone, cream cheese, icing sugar, vanilla extract and lemon zest to a large bowl and whisk together until smooth.

7 Stir in 75ml of the sloe gin then spoon the mixture into the baking tin and use a spatula to spread it evenly over the base. Refrigerate overnight.

8 Make the topping by mixing the blackcurrant jam with the remaining 25ml of sloe gin and the regular gin.

9 Remove the cheesecake from the fridge and the tin, drizzle with the sloe gin and blackcurrant glaze, and serve.

The sweet, thick sloe gin makes this a great winter-time dessert.

Gin & Lemon Scones

Ingredients

- **300g/11oz self-raising flour**
- **60g/2½oz unsalted butter, cubed**
- **40g/1½ oz caster sugar**
- **½ tsp baking powder**

- **½ tsp salt**
- **Zest of 1 lemon**
- **175ml/6 floz gin**
- **60g/2½ oz icing sugar**

Method

1 Preheat the oven to 220°C/425°F/Gas Mark 7. Lightly grease a baking tray.

2 In a large bowl, rub together the flour and butter to create bread crumbs.

3 Mix in the sugar, baking powder, salt and lemon zest.

4 Add the gin, and combine with your hands to form a dough.

5 Pat the dough into a flat circle approx. 5cm/2" thick. Use a round cutter to make 8 evenly-sized scones.

6 Place the scones on the pre-greased baking tray, and bake in the oven for 15 minutes or until risen and golden. Serve warm.

Try these tasty gin and lemon scones with raspberry or gooseberry jam and clotted cream for a special treat.

Gin & Tonic Jellies

Ingredients

- **200g/7oz sugar**
- **600ml/1 pint water**
- **8 leaves leaf gelatine**

- **220ml/7½ floz gin**
- **300ml/10½ floz tonic water**
- **1 lemon, sliced thinly**

Method

1 Heat the sugar and 500ml of the water in a saucepan until the sugar dissolves.

2 Bring to the boil and simmer for 5 minutes.

3 Meanwhile place the remaining 100ml of water in a small, heatproof bowl, and snip in the gelatine. Allow to soak for 10 minutes, then heat over a saucepan of simmering water until the gelatine has dissolved.

4 Mix the dissolved gelatine with the sugar syrup, gin and tonic water in the pan.

5 Divide the mixture between 8 small tumbler glasses.

6 Chill in the fridge for 1 hour, then add a thin slice of lemon to each glass and return to the fridge to set fully.

Try making these gin and tonic jellies in shot glasses instead for the perfect party starter!

Gin Popcorn

Ingredients

- **75g/3oz sweet & salted popcorn**
- **200g/7oz sugar**
- **50g/2oz butter**

- **100ml/3½ floz double cream**
- **25ml/1 floz gin**

Method

1 Heat the sugar in a pan over a medium-high heat until it thickens.

2 Add the butter and whisk, then mix in the double cream.

3 Bring to the boil, then remove from the heat and mix in the gin.

4 Place the popcorn in bowl, pour over the gin sauce, mix around until every piece of popcorn is covered. Serve straight away.

If you like gin, and you like popcorn, we guarantee you'll love this. It's a match made in heaven!

Elderflower Gin Sorbet

Ingredients

- **75g/3oz caster sugar**
- **175ml/6 floz undiluted elderflower cordial**
- **75ml/2½ floz gin**
- **450ml/15½ floz sparkling water**
- **Juice of ½ lemon**
- **1 egg white, beaten**

Method

1 Heat the sugar and elderflower cordial over a medium heat until the sugar dissolves.

2 Allow to cool, then mix in the gin, sparkling water and lemon juice.

3 Transfer to a container and place in the freezer for 2 hours, until the outer edges start to solidify.

4 Stir in the egg white.

5 Place the container back in the freezer for 1 hour. Remove, whisk the sorbet, then place back in the freezer and repeat after another hour.

6 Freeze overnight, then serve the sorbet in cocktail glasses.

This sorbet is light, summery and refreshing. As with many of these recipes, the better the quality of gin you use, the better the results.

Gin & Lemon Curd

Ingredients

- **Zest and juice of 2 lemons**
- **100g/3½ oz sugar**
- **50g/2oz unsalted butter**
- **25ml/1 floz gin**
- **2 eggs, beaten**

Method

1 Place the lemon juice and zest, sugar, butter and gin in a heatproof bowl over a pan of simmering water.

2 Stir continuously until the butter has fully melted.

3 Gradually whisk in the beaten egg, and keep whisking until the mixture thickens.

4 Sieve the mixture into a clean jam jar, to remove the zest.

5 Store in the fridge, and consume within 2 weeks.

Lemon curd is a versatile preserve, and this gin-flavoured version is no different. Spread it on toast, scones, pancakes or even mix with ice cream!

Gin & Tonic Ice Cream

Ingredients

- 200g/7oz sugar
- 60ml/2 floz gin
- 120ml/4 floz tonic

- 25ml/1 floz fresh lemon juice
- 600ml/1 pint double cream
- Lemon slices, to serve

Method

1 Place the sugar in a large mixing bowl, then add the gin, tonic and lemon juice. Stir until the sugar starts to dissolve.

2 Add the cream, and whisk until it has the appearance of an ice cream milkshake.

3 Pour the mixture into a container, and leave in the freezer overnight to freeze.

4 Serve with the lemon wedges, and an extra drizzle of gin.

This delicious dessert is a G&T in ice cream form! You may find the gin makes it softer than regular, non-alcoholic ice cream.

Gin Poached Pears

Serves 4

Ingredients

- **60ml/2 floz gin**
- **60g/2½ oz sugar**
- **600ml/1 pint water**
- **Rind of 1 lemon**

- **Sprig rosemary**
- **Sprig thyme**
- **4 green pears, peeled, cored & halved**

Method

1 Place the gin, sugar, water, lemon rind, rosemary and thyme in a pan over a medium heat, and simmer.

2 Submerge the pears fully in the syrup mixture.

3 Poach the pears for 10-15 minutes, until tender.

4 Serve hot, with some of the poaching syrup drizzled over.

The sharpness of the gin counteracts the sweetness of the pears in this perfectly balanced, deliciously sticky dessert.

Gin Gummy Bears

Ingredients

- **1.5kg/3lb 6oz gummy bears, eg. Haribo**
- **1 litre/1½ pints gin**

Method

1 Place the gummy bears in a bowl.

2 Pour over with gin until all the bears are fully submerged.

3 Leave overnight to allow the bears to soak up the gin. They will expand in size.

4 Serve the next day.

A low or mid-range gin is fine for this recipe, as you won't taste it too much over the flavour of the gummy sweets – just enough to give them a twang!

— Gin —
Cocktails

Classic G&T

Ingredients

- **Ice cubes**
- **60ml/2 fl oz gin**

- **120ml/4 fl oz tonic**
- **Lime wedge**

Method

1 Fill a highball glass with ice cubes.

2 Add the gin, and pour over the tonic.

3 Garnish with the wedge of lime on the side of the glass.

4 Serve immediately.

Gin and tonic is an absolute classic, and whilst using a quality gin is a 'given', more and more people are coming to realise that choosing the right tonic is equally crucial when creating the perfect G & T.

Instead of settling for the standard sweetness and tingle of a supermarket mixer try upgrading to one of the new breed of artisan tonics which offer everything from summery hints of citrus, to herbal notes, Italian bitters and aromas of rosemary and thyme.

Sloe Gin

Ingredients

- **1 litre/1½ pints gin**
- **500g/1lb 2oz sloes**
- **250g/9oz caster sugar**

Method

1 First, place the sloes in a freezer bag and freeze them overnight. This will rupture the sloes' skin, allowing the flavour to seep out into the gin.

2 Place the sloes and sugar in a large jar and pour over the gin.

3 Seal and shake the jar.

4 Store the jar in a cool, dark place, such as a kitchen cupboard or garage, for 3 months.

5 For the first week, shake the jar daily. Thereafter, shake it weekly.

6 After 3 months, strain the mixture through filter paper. Your sloe gin is now ready to drink, but can also be stored indefinitely – it is commonly believed that the longer you leave sloe gin, the better it will taste.

Sloes appear along British hedgerows from September to November. Strike early to ensure your Sloe Gin is ready in time for Christmas!

Gin Mojito

Ingredients

- **60ml/2 floz gin**
- **3 lime wedges**
- **1 tbsp sugar**
- **Handful mint**
- **Crushed ice**
- **Soda water**

Method

1 Add the gin, 2 lime wedges, sugar and a few mint leaves to a highball glass, and stir well.

2 Fill the glass with crushed ice.

3 Top up with soda water.

4 Garnish the glass with a sprig of mint and the third lime wedge.

5 Serve immediately.

This gin-based mojito is a refreshing take on a traditional rum cocktail. To make a raspberry version, add 4 or 5 raspberries to the initial gin mix, and muddle well to release the flavour.

Gin Fizz

Ingredients

- **25ml/1 floz gin**
- **Champagne**

- **Lemon rind**
- **Strawberries, to serve**

Method

1 Chill a champagne flute in the fridge or with ice.

2 Add the gin, and top with the champagne.

3 Garnish the glass with a curl of lemon rind.

4 Serve with fresh strawberries on the side.

The perfect celebratory cocktail, this fizzy little number is great for birthdays, weddings and parties. You may even find it goes down a little too well!

Gin Elderflower Royale

Ingredients

- 60ml/2 floz gin
- 25ml/1 floz sugar syrup
- 25ml/1 floz lemon juice
- 15ml/½ f oz elderflower cordial

- Ice cubes
- Sparkling wine
- Sprig of thyme, to garnish

Method

1 Pour the gin, sugar syrup, lemon juice and elderflower into a cocktail shaker, and mix well.

2 Fill a tall glass half full with ice cubes.

3 Pour in the gin mixture, and top with sparkling wine.

4 Garnish with the thyme sprig, and serve.

Sweet, floral & fizzy - if ever there was a drink that epitomises summer, this is it!

Martini

Ingredients

- **60ml/2 floz gin**
- **25ml/1 floz vermouth**
- **Green olives, to garnish**

Method

1 Pour the gin and vermouth into a cocktail shaker, and mix well.

2 Strain into a frozen martini glass.

3 Garnish with 2 or 3 green olives on a cocktail stick.

There are many different variations of the 'perfect' martini, but the key to every great one is to use high quality gin. Oh, and to serve it shaken, not stirred, of course.

Sloe Gin Spritz

Ingredients

- **60ml/2 floz sloe gin**
- **25ml/1 floz lemon juice**
- **25ml/1 floz sugar syrup**
- **25ml/1 floz egg whites**
- **Sprig of rosemary**

Method

1 Add the sloe gin, lemon juice, sugar syrup and egg whites into a cocktail shaker, and mix until frothy.

2 Pour into a frozen wine glass.

3 Garnish with the sprig of rosemary.

Perhaps a more wintery cocktail than the others, this Sloe Gin Fizz is sweet, thick and frothy, and makes a great addition to Christmas parties

Strawberry Gin Lemonade

Serves 1

Ingredients

- **Ice cubes**
- **25ml/1 floz gin**
- **60ml/2 floz lemonade**
- **2 strawberries**
- **4 basil leaves**
- **Soda water**

Method

1 In a cocktail shaker, add the ice, gin and lemonade, and mix well.

2 Add 1 strawberry and the basil leaves to a glass, and gently mash. Fill with ice.

3 Pour the gin and lemonade over the muddled strawberry and basil, and top with soda water.

4 Garnish with the remaining strawberry, and serve.

Try serving this fruity lemonade in old-fashioned mason jars to complete the vintage feel.

Bramble

Ingredients

- **60ml/2 floz dry gin**
- **25ml/1 floz lemon juice**
- **15ml/½ floz sugar syrup**
- **15ml/½ floz Crème de Mure**

- **Crushed ice**
- **Blackberries, to garnish**
- **Lemon wedge, to garnish**

Method

1 In a cocktail shaker, mix the gin, lemon juice and sugar syrup.

2 Strain into a glass filled with crushed ice.

3 Pour the Crème de Mure over the top.

4 Garnish the glass with a blackberry and lemon wedge.

Did you know? This blackberry flavoured cocktail was originally created by famous barman Dick Bradsell, who also invented the Espresso Martini.

Bee's Knees

Ingredients

- **60ml/2 floz dry gin**
- **2 tsp honey**
- **25ml/1 floz orange juice**
- **25ml/1 floz lemon juice**
- **Orange peel, to garnish**

Method

1 In a cocktail shaker, mix the gin and honey until the honey has dissolved.

2 Add the orange and lemon juices, fill with ice, and shake.

3 Strain into a pre-chilled glass.

4 Garnish with the orange peel, and serve.

If you find this delicious concoction a little too sweet for your tastes, try serving it over ice to dilute it slightly.

Rose Gin Fizz

Ingredients

- **60ml/2 floz dry gin**
- **25ml/1 floz double cream**
- **1 egg white**
- **15ml/½ floz lemon juice**
- **15ml/½ floz lime juice**
- **1 tsp grenadine**

- **15ml/½ floz sugar syrup (equal parts sugar and water)**
- **2 drops rose water**
- **Ice**
- **Soda water**
- **Rose petals, to garnish**

Method

1 Pour the gin, double cream, egg white, lime, lemon, sugar syrup, grenadine and rose water into a cocktail shaker, and shake hard for 30 seconds.

2 Add ice to the cocktail shaker, and shake again for 30 seconds.

3 Strain into a tall glass, and top with soda water.

4 Garnish with rose petals, and serve.

This rosy cocktail is sweet and creamy - the perfect after-dinner treat. Make it with orange blossom water instead of rose water for the classic Ramos Gin Fizz.

Long Island Iced Tea

Ingredients

- **15ml/½ floz gin**
- **15ml/½ floz vodka**
- **15ml/½ floz rum**
- **15ml/½ floz tequila**
- **15ml/½ floz Triple Sec (or similar orange liqueur)**
- **15ml/½ floz lemon juice**
- **1tsp sugar syrup (equal parts sugar and water)**
- **Ice**
- **Cola**
- **Lemon slice, to garnish**

Method

1 Pour the gin, vodka, rum, tequila, Triple Sec, lemon juice and sugar syrup into a cocktail shaker, add ice and shake vigorously.

2 Pour into pre-chilled glass and top up with a splash of cola.

3 Garnish with the lemon, and serve.

*This is a serious cocktail.
Be careful not to over indulge.*

Earl Grey Martini

Ingredients

- **60ml/2 floz gin**
- **40ml/1½ floz cold Earl Grey tea**
- **25ml/1 floz lemon juice**
- **½ egg white**
- **15ml/½ floz sugar syrup (equal parts sugar and water)**
- **Lemon peel, to garnish**

Method

1 Pour the gin, Earl Grey tea, lemon juice and sugar syrup to a cocktail shaker and shake well.

2 Add ice to the cocktail shaker, and mix again.

3 Strain into a martini glass.

4 Garnish with the lemon peel, and serve.

Floral Earl Grey mixed with fragrant gin makes this a deliciously sophisticated cocktail.

Ruby Sipper

Ingredients

- **60ml/2 floz gin**
- **25ml/1 floz sugar syrup (equal parts sugar and water)**
- **25ml/1 floz Triple Sec (or similar orange liqueur)**
- **25ml/1 floz lemon juice**
- **15ml/½ floz Crème de cassis**
- **15ml/½ floz Campari**
- **Orange zest, to garnish**

Method

1 Add all the ingredients other than the orange zest to a cocktail shaker, and mix well.

2 Pour into a goblet glass.

3 Garnish with the orange zest, and serve.

This refreshing cocktail is full of citrus and berry notes, and makes a great alternative to Pimm's at summer garden parties.

Singapore Sling

Ingredients

- 60ml/2 floz gin
- 15ml/½ floz cherry liqueur
- 7ml/¼ floz Benedictine (or similar herbal liqueur)
- 7ml/¼ floz Triple Sec (or similar orange liqueur)
- 120ml/4 fl oz pineapple juice

- 15ml/½ floz lime juice
- 7ml/¼ floz grenadine
- Ice
- Soda water
- Orange slice, to garnish
- Cherry, to garnish

Method

1 Add the gin, cherry liqueur, Benedictine, Triple Sec, pineapple juice, lime juice and grenadine to a cocktail shaker with ice and shake well.

2 Pour into a pre-chilled highball glass.

3 Top with a splash of soda water.

4 Garnish with the orange slice and cherry, and serve.

Did you know? The creation of the Singapore Sling is attributed to Ngiam Tong Boon, barman at the Raffles Hotel in Singapore, sometime around 1915.

Gimlet

Ingredients

- **60ml/2 floz gin**
- **15ml/½ floz lime juice**

- **15ml/½ fl oz sugar syrup**
- **Lime peel, to garnish**

Method

1 Half fill a glass with ice.

2 Add the gin, lime juice and sugar syrup, and stir.

3 Garnish with the lime peel, and serve.

This sweet, citrusy cocktail is perfect for summer - use a high quality gin for best results.

Rhubarb Gin Sour

Ingredients

- **100g/3½oz rhubarb, chopped**
- **200g/7oz sugar**
- **250ml/8½ floz water**
- **25ml/1 floz gin**
- **25ml/1 floz lemon juice**
- **1 egg white**
- **Ice**

Method

1 First, make a rhubarb syrup by putting the rhubarb, sugar and water in a saucepan.

2 Bring to the boil, then simmer over a low heat, stirring continuously for 10-15 minutes.

3 Remove the rhubarb pieces and measure 120ml/4fl oz of the syrup for use in the cocktail (save the rest for the next one!)

4 Pour the rhubarb syrup, gin, lemon juice and egg white into a cocktail shaker with ice and shake vigorously for 30 seconds.

5 Strain the cocktail into a glass filled with crushed ice.

The pretty pink colour of this tasty cocktail makes it a perfect choice for Valentine's Day – why not whip a couple up to go with your romantic meal?

Negroni

Ingredients

- **25ml/1 floz gin**
- **25ml/1 floz red vermouth**
- **25ml/1 floz Campari**

- **Ice**
- **Orange peel, to garnish**

Method

1 Add all ingredients to a cocktail shaker with ice, and mix well.

2 Strain into a glass filled with ice cubes.

3 Garnish with orange peel, and serve.

The Campari can make this cocktail quite bitter – if it's too much for you, alter the ratios and include less Campari and more vermouth.

Monkey Gland

Ingredients

- **60ml/2 floz gin**
- **60ml/2 floz fresh orange juice**
- **1 tsp absinthe**
- **1 tsp grenadine**
- **Ice**
- **Orange peel, to garnish**

Method

1 Pour all the ingredients into a cocktail shaker, and shake vigorously.

2 Strain into a chilled cocktail glass.

3 Garnish with the orange peel, and serve.

For best results, make sure you use high quality ingredients, especially freshly squeezed orange juice.

Gin Buck

Serves 1

Ingredients

- **60ml/2 floz gin**
- **½ lime, juiced**

- **60ml/2 floz ginger ale**
- **Lime wedge, to garnish**

Method

1 Add the gin and lime juice to a glass filled with ice, and stir.

2 Top with the ginger ale.

3 Garnish with the lime wedge, and serve.

This refreshing drink can also be made with lemon juice, instead of lime, if you prefer.

Gin Corpse Reviver No.2

Ingredients

- ½ tsp absinthe
- 25ml/1 floz gin
- 25ml/1floz white vermouth
- 25ml/1floz fresh lemon juice
- 25ml/1floz Triple Sec (or similar orange liqueur)
- Ice
- Lemon peel, to garnish

Method

1 Use the absinthe to a rinse a chilled cocktail glass.

2 Add the gin, vermouth, Triple Sec and lemon juice to a cocktail shaker with ice, and shake well.

3 Strain into the pre-rinsed cocktail glass.

4 Garnish with the lemon peel, and serve.

The No.2 is part of a collection of cocktails known as the 'Corpse Reviver', created as a hangover cure (hence the morbid name!)

Tom Collins

Ingredients

- Ice
- 60ml/2 floz gin
- 25ml/1 floz lemon juice
- 60ml/2 floz soda water
- 15ml/½ floz sugar syrup (equal parts sugar and water)
- Lemon wedge, to garnish

Method

1 Fill a Collins glass with ice cubes.

2 Add the gin, lemon juice and sugar syrup, and stir thoroughly.

3 Top with the soda water.

4 Garnish with the lemon wedge, and serve.

The origins of the Tom Collins cocktail date back to the 1800s. To make a classic version, try using Old Tom or Plymouth gin, as this is likely what they would have used back then.

Aviation

Ingredients

- **60ml/2 floz gin**
- **15ml/½ floz Maschino liqueur**
- **15ml/½ floz Crème de Violette**
- **25ml/1 floz lemon juice**
- **Ice**
- **Cherry**

Method

1 Add the gin, Maschino liqueur, Crème de Violette and lemon juice to a cocktail shaker with ice, and mix well.

2 Strain into a cocktail glass.

3 Garnish with the cherry, and serve.

Crème de Violette isn't the most common liqueur, but it's worth tracking down for its fantastic violet colour – this cocktail is a real showstopper.

Blueberry Gin Sour

Ingredients

- **50g/2oz blueberries**
- **25ml/1 floz lemon juice**
- **15ml/½ floz sugar syrup (equal parts sugar and water)**
- **60ml/2 floz gin**
- **1 tbsp egg white**
- **Ice**
- **Blueberries, to garnish**

Method

1 Place the blueberries, lemon juice and sugar syrup into a glass, and muddle well.

2 Strain the mixture into a cocktail shaker using a sieve, pressing the juices out using the back of a spoon.

3 Add the gin and egg white to the shaker, and mix thoroughly.

4 Strain the cocktail into a glass filled with ice.

5 Garnish with blueberries, and serve.

This tangy, fruity cocktail is perfect for blueberry lovers, and makes a delicious way to get a little of your 5-a-day!

Vesper Martini

Ingredients

- **75ml/2½ floz Gordon's gin**
- **25ml/1 floz vodka**
- **15ml/½ floz Lillet Blanc**

- **Ice**
- **Lemon peel, to garnish**

Method

1 Add the gin, vodka and Lillet Blanc to a cocktail shaker with ice, and shake until ice-cold.

2 Strain into a pre-chilled martini glass.

3 Garnish with lemon peel, and serve.

This drink first appeared in Ian Fleming's novel Casino Royale, as James Bond's own creation. The original recipe calls for Kina Lillet, but this is no longer available, so Lillet Blanc dry vermouth is substituted.

Floradora

Ingredients

- **60ml/2 floz gin**
- **25ml/1 floz lime juice**
- **25ml/1 floz Crème de Framboise (or similar raspberry liqueur)**

- **Ice**
- **120ml/4 floz ginger beer**
- **Raspberries, to garnish**
- **Lime wedge**

Method

1 Pour the gin, lime juice and Crème de Framboise into a cocktail shaker with ice, and shake well.

2 Strain into a large glass filled with ice.

3 Top up with ginger beer.

4 Garnish with the raspberries and lime wedge, and serve.

This seductive pink cocktail was inspired by a popular musical comedy which debuted in the West End in 1899, and had a cast of six beautiful women, known as 'The Floradora Sextette'.

Strawberry Gin Daiquiri

Ingredients

- 60ml/2 floz gin
- 25ml/1 floz fresh lime juice
- 5 large strawberries
- 4 ice cubes

Method

1 Add all ingredients to a blender, and mix until the ice is crushed.

2 Pour into a pre-chilled martini glass.

3 Serve immediately.

This gin variation on the popular rum drink is the grown-up version of a strawberry slush – but tastes even better!

Gin-Gin Mule

Ingredients

- **15ml/½ floz sugar syrup (equal parts sugar and water)**
- **15ml/½ floz fresh lime juice**
- **Handful of mint leaves**

- **60ml/2 floz gin**
- **Ice**
- **25ml/1 floz ginger beer**
- **Sprig of mint, to garnish**

Method

1 In a cocktail shaker, first muddle the sugar syrup, lime juice and mint leaves.

2 Add the gin and a handful of ice, and shake well.

3 Pour into a tall glass filled with ice.

4 Top with ginger beer, and stir.

5 Garnish with the sprig of mint, and serve.

This long cocktail is the very definition of refreshing. Try adding slices of fresh lime before serving to make it more citrusy.

Blue Lady

Ingredients

- **60ml/2 floz gin**
- **60ml/2 floz lemon juice**
- **25ml/1 floz blue curacao**

- **Ice**
- **Cherry, to garnish**

Method

1 Add the gin, lemon juice and blue curacao to a cocktail shaker with ice, and shake well.

2 Strain into a pre-chilled cocktail glass.

3 Garnish with the cherry, and serve.

To make this sour cocktail sweeter, you could add sugar to the rim of the glass by moistening it with lemon or lime juice, and then dipping it in sugar.

Colour Changing Gin

Ingredients

- **250ml/8½ floz gin**
- **6 dried butterfly pea flowers**

Method

1 Pour the gin into a clean jar.

2 Add the dried butterfly pea flowers, screw on the lid and shake well.

3 Leave to infuse overnight.

4 Once the gin has turned purple in colour, strain into a bottle. Discard the used pea flowers.

5 Store in a cool place until needed.

The purplish-blue colour of this gin is pretty impressive in itself, but the real magic happens when you add it to lemon or lime juice – the citrus will make the gin turn pink.

Pomegranate & Rosemary Gin Fizz

Ingredients

- 60ml/2 floz gin
- 60ml/2 floz pomegranate juice
- 25ml/1 floz lemon juice
- 25ml/1 floz sugar syrup (equal parts sugar and water)

- Ice
- Soda water
- Pomegranate seeds, to garnish
- Rosemary sprig, to garnish

Method

1 Add the gin, pomegranate, lemon juice and sugar syrup to a cocktail shaker with ice and mix well.

2 Strain into a glass over ice.

3 Garnish with the pomegranates and rosemary sprig, and serve.

Pomegranates are a super food, so this fruity cocktail will combat any negative effects of the gin... right?

Peach G&T

Ingredients

- Ice
- ½ peach, cut into wedges
- 60ml/2 floz gin
- 120ml/4 floz tonic water
- 25ml/1 floz freshly squeezed lime juice
- Lime wedges, to garnish

Method

1 Fill a glass with ice and the peach wedges.

2 Add the gin, tonic water and lime juice, and stir.

3 Garnish with the lime wedges, and serve immediately.

This drink is 2-in-1 – a light and refreshing cocktail, with a delicious gin-soaked peach snack afterwards!

Mulled Gin

Ingredients

- 1 litre/1½ pints gin
- 275g/10oz sugar
- 1 cinnamon stick

- 6 whole cloves
- 6 cardamom pods
- 1 vanilla pod

Method

1 Heat a pan on a low heat and stir in 250ml of the gin and sugar until the sugar dissolves.

2 Bring to the boil for 2 minutes.

3 Pour into a large jar, add the remaining gin, cinnamon, cloves and vanilla, and stir.

4 Leave to cool, then seal the jar and store in a cool, dark place for 1 month.

5 Sieve through kitchen paper into a clean jar and serve as desired.

This warm and spicy gin makes a great alternative to mulled wine around Christmas time.

Kiwi Gin Fizz

Ingredients

- 1 tsp honey
- 25ml/1 floz gin
- 1 slice of kiwi

- Ice
- Soda water

Method

1 Add the honey, gin and kiwi to a glass.

2 Fill the glass with ice.

3 Top up with soda water and serve.

A zingy take on a classic gin and soda, the kiwi and honey are subtle flavours which will not detract from the taste of the gin.

Hibiscus Flower Gin Sour

Ingredients

- **200g/7oz caster sugar**
- **250ml/8½ floz water**
- **40g/2½ oz dried hibiscus flowers**
- **100ml/3½ floz gin**
- **25ml/1 floz lemon juice**
- **1 egg white**
- **Ice**

Method

1 First, make a hibiscus syrup by heating the sugar, water and hibiscus flowers in a pan over a low heat until the sugar has dissolved. Remove from heat and allow to cool.

2 Measure out 25ml/1 fl oz for use in the cocktail. The remaining syrup can be stored in a bottle or jar for use later.

3 Add the hibiscus syrup, gin, lemon and egg white to a cocktail shaker with ice, and shake vigorously for 30 seconds.

4 Strain into a cocktail glass, and serve.

Garnish with more hibiscus flowers and wild flower petals for a truly Instagram-worthy drink.

Serves 1

Skittles Gin

Ingredients

- **5 large bags of skittles**
- **1 litre/1½ pints gin**
- **Tonic water, to serve**

Method

1 Open the bags of skittles and separate them by colour.

2 Place the sweets of each colour into a clean bottle or jam jar.

3 Top up each jar with gin, seal the lid and shake well.

4 Place jars in the fridge for 2 days to infuse.

5 Strain the coloured gin through cheesecloth into new, fresh jars to remove lumps.

6 Store the finished jars in a cool, dark place until required. To serve, pour 60ml/2 fl oz of the skittles gin over ice in a glass, and top with a splash of tonic.

This recipe can be adapted for a variety of other sweets – how about Starburst or Parma Violets flavoured gin?

Try these bonus glamorous Prosecco recipes from **the Prosecco cookbook**

Prosecco Chicken

Ingredients

- 2 tbsp olive oil
- 3 tbsp plain flour
- Salt & pepper
- 1 tbsp orange zest
- 1.35kg/3lb chicken, quartered
- 150g/5oz pancetta, diced
- 12 shallots, peeled & halved

- 1 red chilli, seeded and finely chopped
- 2 tsp rosemary, chopped
- 1 bottle Prosecco
- Fresh rosemary sprigs, to garnish

Method

1 Heat the olive oil in a large pan. Season the flour with salt, pepper and orange zest, then toss the chicken pieces in the flour mix until they're thoroughly coated.

2 Brown the coated chicken pieces in the pan, skin-side down, in batches if necessary. Transfer the chicken to a plate.

3 Throw the pancetta into the pan and cook until crisp. Reduce the heat. Add the shallots, chilli and rosemary and sauté for about 5 minutes.

4 Return the chicken to the pan. Pour the Prosecco over the top and simmer for 25 -30 minutes, until the sauce becomes syrupy and the chicken is all thoroughly cooked.

5 Season with salt and pepper and serve garnished with sprigs of fresh rosemary.

Enjoy with salad, and a fresh glass of Prosecco!

Try these bonus glamorous Prosecco recipes from **the Prosecco cookbook**

Prosecco & Prawn Risotto

Ingredients

- **1kg/2¼ lb king prawns**
- **1lt/4 cups stock**
- **100g/3½oz unsalted butter**
- **Salt & pepper**

- **1 onion, peeled and finely chopped**
- **350g/12oz risotto rice**
- **250ml/1 cup Prosecco**

Method

1 Clean and shell the prawns.

2 In a frying pan melt about a third of the butter until it begins to bubble. Add the prawns and sauté for two minutes. Season and remove from the heat.

3 In a different frying pan, melt the remaining butter and fry the onion until soft. Add the rice and cook for a minute or two, stirring.

4 Pour in the Prosecco and cook, stirring constantly until it begins to reduce. Ladle in the hot stock, adding more as soon as it's absorbed. Repeat for about 20 minutes or until the rice is al dente.

5 Stir in the prawns and cook until pink and piping hot. Taste and adjust the seasoning and stock if necessary.

6 Remove the risotto from the heat and serve immediately.

Truly creamy & delicious, washed down with the remaining Prosecco!

Try these bonus glamorous Prosecco recipes from **the Prosecco cookbook**

Prosecco Turkey Meatballs

Ingredients

- 450g/1lb minced turkey
- ½ onion, peeled and finely chopped
- 1 rice cake, crumbled
- 1 egg
- ½ tsp salt

- Ground black pepper
- 75g/3oz tomato puree
- 200g/7oz cranberries, fresh or frozen
- ½ tsp Dijon mustard
- 250ml/1 cup Prosecco

Method

1 Preheat the oven to 400F/200C/Gas6

2 Throw the turkey, onion and crumbled rice cake into a large bowl. Break in the egg and season with salt and pepper. Mix it all together with your hands. Shape it into 12 small meatballs and place each on a lined baking sheet.

3 Bake in the oven for 15-20 minutes or until cooked through.

4 Pour the tomato puree, cranberries, mustard and Prosecco into a large pan and cook on high heat until boiling.

5 Add the baked meatballs and stir to coat them thoroughly. Lower the heat and simmer, uncovered for 10 minutes.

6 Lovely served with pasta or rice.

Ideal as a festive starter or make fewer, larger meatballs for a main course.

Prosecco Oysters & Turbot

Ingredients

- **8 oysters, opened with juices retained**
- **1 shallot, peeled and shredded**
- **250ml/1 cup Prosecco**
- **2 tbsp double cream**
- **100g/3½oz butter**

- **Squeeze of lemon juice**
- **Salt & pepper**
- **4 turbot fillets, skinned**
- **1 large leek, finely shredded**
- **1 tbsp chervil, chopped**

Method

1 In a pan, gently warm the oysters in their juices for a couple of minutes. Remove from the heat.

2 In a different pan, heat the shallot with the Prosecco. Bring to the boil, and reduce the liquid by about half. Strain the oyster juice into the pan, and continuing to boil until the liquid reduces by another half. Pour in the cream and when it's simmering again, whisk in about three quarters of the butter, a little at a time. Add a squeeze of lemon juice, and season with salt and pepper. Set aside.

3 Divide the remaining butter between two frying pans and place both over medium heat. Once sizzling, place the turbot in one pan and the shredded leek in the other. Season both with salt and freshly ground black pepper. Fry until the turbot becomes light golden, then turn it. Cook the leek until softened.

4 Re-warm the sauce, and add the oysters and chervil. Divide the leeks between four bowls, and arrange the turbot and oysters on top. Spoon the Prosecco sauce over everything.

5 Serve immediately.

Enjoy this luxurious main course with a glass of chilled Prosecco.

You may also enjoy....

A comical collection of quotes for gin devotees, prosecco princesses, wine aficionados and beer lovers.

In a world where moderation or even abstention of our favourite tipple has all but curbed our joy, we bring you a light hearted, comical collection of quotes, sayings, mantras and truisms that confirm what you already knew to be true.... that gin, prosecco, wine & beer are good for you!